T0105692

Forgiveness

Our Greatest Need, Our Greatest Gift

Dr. George W. Mitchell

Pastor/Teacher

WestBow
PRESS
A DIVISION OF THOMAS NELSON

WestBow Press books may be ordered through booksellers or by contacting:

WestBow Press
A Division of Thomas Nelson
1663 Liberty Drive
Bloomington, IN 47403
www.westbowpress.com
1-(866) 928-1240

Because of the dynamic nature of the Internet, any web addresses or
links contained in this book may have changed since publication and
may no longer be valid. The views expressed in this work are solely those
of the author and do not necessarily reflect the views of the publisher,
and the publisher hereby disclaims any responsibility for them.

Any people depicted in stock imagery provided by Thinkstock are models,
and such images are being used for illustrative purposes only.
Certain stock imagery © Thinkstock.

ISBN: 978-1-4497-7025-9 (e)
ISBN: 978-1-4497-7026-6 (sc)

Library of Congress Control Number: 2012919825

Printed in the United States of America

WestBow Press rev. date: 10/24/2012

To the men who have been my friends and accountability partners and who have been committed to cause me to be a man of God, living faithfully in this world: Bo Stalcup, C. Phil Esty, John Tolson, Rob Danner, Shelton Sanford, Boyce Callahan, Roy Flannagan, Matt Burton, George Taylor, Huck Whitener, Tom Cheely, Roy Blankenship, Bill Griffin, Carl Harris, Brian Scott, and last, but not least, my two sons: Caleb and Stephen. Thanks, men, for always challenging me and always offering me freely your forgiveness.

Contents

Introduction

No forgiveness means no relationship.

No forgiveness means no hope.

No forgiveness means no comfort.

No forgiveness means no encouragement.

No forgiveness means no rest.

No forgiveness means no patience.

No forgiveness means no peace.

No forgiveness means no joy.

No forgiveness means no grace.

No forgiveness means no mercy.

No forgiveness means no love.

No forgiveness means no gentleness.

No forgiveness means no kindness.

No forgiveness means no forgiveness.

The above list could go on and on. Forgiveness is essential to our living in a world that seems to always be sucking the life out of us.

Often, we are unforgiving people living in the midst of unforgiving people. For many of us, this is why we lack healthy relationships, hope, comfort, encouragement, rest, patience, peace, joy, grace, mercy, love, gentleness, kindness, and many other attributes that we long to possess.

Matthew 9 tells us a story of a man who is a paralytic. Four of his friends have carried this man on his pallet to see Jesus. They want Jesus to heal their friend. We are not told how old this man is or how long he has been paralyzed. It would appear that he was probably in his late twenties or early thirties and that he had been paralyzed most of his life, probably from birth. His friends are so intent on helping this man that when they can't bring him through the front door because of the crowd, they go up the back stairs to the flat roof and dig a hole through the clay. Then they lower the man by ropes attached to the pallet so that he comes to rest in front of Jesus.

As Jesus looks at this man, it is obvious that this man needs his physical strength returned and life given to his dead limbs. There is no question that this is what is going to restore manhood to this individual; this is what is going to give him his worth and value; this is what is going to give this man a reason to live, to rise up in the morning with the hope of going to work so he can provide for himself and his family. Jesus looks at this man, and what does He say? With all sincerity, Jesus says, "Take courage, son, your sins are forgiven" (Matthew 9:2b). What? How absurd! How ridiculous! How utterly blind can Jesus be to this man's need! Does He not understand that these men have brought their friend to be healed? Is He oblivious to this man's feelings? He has just denied these feelings of utter despair that must be filling both the heart of the paralytic and his friends.

What is Jesus doing? He is refocusing this man's thinking, as well as everyone else's, to recognize that this man's greatest need is not his physical paralysis but his inward corruption. What he needs to know above all is that his sins are forgiven. Now to show everyone there that Jesus, in fact, has the right and power to forgive sins, He restores the man's ability to walk, to run, to go to the restroom on his own, to feed himself, to dress himself, to find work, and to do all the things that we take for granted because we are not paralyzed. However, no matter how glorious and wonderful all of that seems, it is nothing compared to forgiveness.

Another unforgettable scene in the New Testament is the crucifixion. Jesus' flesh is stripped from His body. He is spat upon, beaten, mocked, and has a crown of thorns set on His head. He is nailed to a cross by His hands and His feet, and the cross is dropped into a hole so that Christ may die an agonizing and painful death. Yet, as he hangs there, with the ability to destroy anyone and everyone who had been involved in His torture, mocking, and crucifixion, He says, "Father, forgive them; for they do not know what they are doing" (Luke 23:34). This says it is forgiveness that will change the punishment that those deserve who have been plotting, betraying, carrying out their schemes and plans against the Lord of glory.

Forgiveness is the key to our relationships and to our own personal health. Then what is it? How do I get it? How do I give it? What keeps me from wanting to give it to others? Peter's age-old question is "How often should I forgive?" (Matthew 18:21). When should I forgive? When is forgiveness not necessary? Is there someone who has not forgiven me? Is there someone who I have not forgiven?

Forgiveness is our greatest need. At the same time, forgiveness is the greatest gift we can receive and it is the greatest gift we can give. Let's look at this enigma and decide whether we are ones who readily give forgiveness or ones who selfishly withhold it.

Just a quick personal note before we begin. I do know what it is to have a person look at you and utter those words that will haunt you and hurt you: "I will never forgive you!" It is like a sharp knife sinking into you and cutting away at your inner soul, slashing and tearing, leaving a gash that continues to bleed and never heals. You really don't know what to do with the pain. The person walks away and you want to reach out, grab him, and pull him back into your sphere of relationships, but you know it is not possible. I have a close friend who is a constant encouragement to me. He has a brother who, at one time, was his partner in business. Something happened; they had a disagreement, a misunderstanding. The brother and other family members only live about thirty minutes away. No matter what my friend does or says, his brother refuses to have anything to do with him. The separation not only affects the two of them, but it affects their extended families. I see the deep hurt in my friend's face and hear it in his voice as he speaks about his brother. Unforgiveness is one of the most destructive forces facing the lives of men and women today.

I also know the unforgiveness that comes when the words are not even spoken. Over the past months, I have experienced the greatest loss of my entire life. It is the most painful thing I have ever known. In some ways, I would have preferred that someone would have literally cut off my right arm. One of the things that has made this so excruciating is the declaration that I am not forgiven, not by words spoken but by utter silence that speaks more loudly than any cry, shout, or scream that I could have ever heard. It is like that rare disease that starts eating away at your flesh and removes your fingers, your hands, your toes, and your feet. It is this slow progression of taking away your strength, your hope, and the very people that you love so dearly. No matter how much you plead and beg and ask for forgiveness, and even seek to change in the way you act and behave, there is no grace given.

There is no word spoken, and the silence comes at you with the force of a ten-ton truck. It leaves you sprawled out on the ground where you are unable to move, and at times even unable to rise up and continue to walk through this life. You feel like that dishrag where all the water has been wrung out and you have been hung up to dry.

Yes, I also know what it is to wonder, "How can I forgive that person for what he has done to me?" He has stripped me of something that I don't think I can ever get back. The feelings that begin to well up overpower us, and it seems that we cannot get rid of them.

My only reason for bringing all this up is to point out my own struggles with forgiveness. I can tell you that involved in all of this have been those emotions of betrayal, false accusations, open rejection, questioning of my own motives, deep hurt, and the pang of being wounded. I have thought, *I am right and everything that has taken place in these instances is wrong, and I have been terribly mistreated.* This kind of thinking has often clouded my whole perspective in regard to forgiveness. Not only have I demanded pardon, but I have thought that I have deserved it. I have had my "pity parties," and I have raged with anger because I can't believe someone is treating me the way that they are. I have wrestled with the very question: what do I do with those who have not forgiven me? So the whole concept of forgiveness has stared me in the face and brought me to the place where I must do battle with it.

If I am going to properly live in this world and even have any kind of impact upon the people around me, I must be a person who understands what forgiveness is and how to give it. I must know forgiveness in my own life. I must know how I can receive forgiveness. Where is it ultimately going to come from? As I receive it, I can give it. However, if I do not get the release from doing wrong to others, how do I give it anyway? Forgiveness is the only thing that can free me up. Especially as I live in relationships, there can only be that closeness and understanding when there is the giving and receiving of pardon and peace.

Think about this! A woman—a sinner, a prostitute—comes to Jesus Christ while He is eating in the house of a Pharisee, a Jewish religious ruler of the first century. She comes with a very expensive jar of perfume and begins to pour it over Jesus' feet, all the time weeping, wiping His feet with her hair, and even kissing His feet (Luke 7:36–38). It is quite a picture. The Pharisee, upon seeing this, rebukes Jesus for letting such a woman do what she is doing (v. 39). Jesus, in explaining His actions, uses a parable that focuses on the whole subject of forgiveness. Verse 49 is the key to the parable: "For this reason I say to you, her sins (referring to the woman who is ministering to Jesus), which are many, have been forgiven, for she loved much; but he who is forgiven little, loves little."

Now let us begin this study. Let us do so knowing *the battle is on!*

Chapter 1

The First Thing

As we begin our fundamental examination of forgiveness, we must know a few things. I do not believe an individual can define forgiveness on his or her own. However, I do believe there is a basic flaw in every person's nature. A person on his or her own cannot just think about the concept of forgiveness and decide the meaning of it, nor can a person look at what others say in the realm of psychology or psychiatry and choose the one concept that best agrees with his or her own analysis. There is basically something wrong with the inner core of every person that causes him or her to look at everything from a self-centered, prideful, self-assertive point of view that darkens and misconstrues everything he or she sees, believes, or thinks.

We are broken. There must be a reliable outside source to tell us what is true. This is why the human race needs a personal, infinite God who reveals true reality. We must have a living word, which is represented in the person and work of Jesus Christ. We also need a written Word that communicates the mind and will of this triune God who makes Himself known to us.

This is the starting point of this whole discussion. I cannot begin to talk about forgiveness by simply presenting my feelings, ideas, or insights. It would be only my guesses, hunches, theories, longings, or desires about what forgiveness is or should be. Therefore, I must rely on the person and work of Christ and His written revelation to mankind to speak about forgiveness and what it is. The truth is not found in my best opinion about the subject. What I do know is that I have, in many ways, misunderstood and failed miserably in giving this great gift to others and in my demand of it from others.

The flaw in me and in you is far more than a little glitch in our character that can be easily fixed. It is something that affects our whole essence. Do you like apples? What is the central part of this fruit? It is the core. What do we normally do with it? Most of the time, we throw it away. Yet it is in this core that the seeds reside, and the seeds determine what kind of apple we are eating.

Every person's core determines what a person thinks, chooses, and feels. God says our core, that place deep within us, is completely tainted. Forgiveness must come from our core, but God's written communication tells us that "not even one, is righteous (that is perfectly lives up to God's standard), seeks after God, or does good" (Romans 3:9–18). In fact, everyone has a mouth with a tongue that is like an open grave, full of cursing, bitterness, and deception with lips that are like a poisonous snake. And we have feet that are quick to step on other people, a walk that brings misery wherever it goes and lacks knowledge of peace and a fear of God "before their eyes."

This describes every person born into the world. Originally, this is what I look like; this is what you look like. So you come into my life. You and I start trying to build a relationship together. As we are doing this, you say or do something that hurts or offends me, which, by the way, is in your very nature to do.

Let's say in this scenario that you even say you are sorry and ask me to forgive you. Where does that come from? It has to come from the core—the place where I think, choose, and feel. Remember what that is! Take a minute and go back and read the last paragraph again.

Let me give you another description of that place deep within. In this core, you and I possess a depraved or corrupt mind that leads us "to do these things which are not proper, *being filled with* [emphasis mine] all unrighteousness, wickedness, greed, malice; *full of* [emphasis mine] envy, murder, strife, deceit, malice; they are gossips, slanderers, boastful, inventors of evil, disobedient to parents, without understanding, untrustworthy, unloving, unmerciful" (Romans 3:28b–31).

This is our problem. If we are trying to forgive each other from our original interests or pleasures, we will fail miserably. We might say, "I forgive you." But if we are plagued with an inner self that is controlled by a self-regulating center, then we don't know what forgiveness is or how to freely give it to someone else. In fact, in most cases, whenever we have the opportunity, it will be payback time. We will present those who have slighted or humiliated us to others in a way that will call into question those people's character and motives. It takes only a word, a look, a rolling of the eyes to say to someone else that he or she should regard the person in question with a less favorable view.

Just one more list to remind us of what oftentimes dominates our actions: "Now the deeds of the flesh (our human motivations and actions) *are evident* [emphasis mine], which are immorality, impurity, sensuality, idolatry, sorcery, enmities, strife, jealousy, outbursts of anger, disputes, dissentions, factions, envying, drunkenness, carousing, and things like these" (Galatians 5:19b–21a). These things fill our minds and pour forth from our lives as a powerful flood meant to wash others away. Look around! What do we read about in the papers? What do we see on television? What do we experience from friends and family? What do friends and family experience from us?

Before we can even talk about forgiveness, something has to happen so that we can comprehend what forgiveness is. What part of our nature affects what we think about others, feel about others, and choose to do toward others when they wound us? This is why it is necessary to have an outside source to tell us what can reshape our inner essence. The personal, infinite God says He will "sprinkle clean water on you; I will cleanse you from all your filthiness and from all your idols. Moreover, I will give you a *new heart* (emphasis mine ["a new core," my words]) and put a new spirit within you; and I will remove the heart of stone from your flesh and give you a heart of flesh. I will put My Spirit within you and cause you to walk in My statutes, and you will be careful to observe My ordinances" (Ezekiel 36:25–27).

This is what God does. It is a supernatural work that happens when we receive righteousness, a perfect life, which comes from God through the instrumentality of faith in Jesus Christ. This is why Jesus Christ came into the world to live a flawless life, die on the cross in our place, be raised from the dead, ascend into heaven, assume the position of King over all the world at the right hand of God, and be in the position of intercessor for those who have and will believe in Him. It is our faith and trust in Him who has accomplished all this for us that entitles us to be given His spirit, which comes to live within us and changes our very makeup.

Radical transformation is what describes this metamorphosis. Such redesign is described as a "new creation," "a new creature" where "old things passed away; behold new things have come" (2 Corinthians 5:17). It is the "law of the Spirit of life in Christ Jesus," "a new principle of life" (Romans 8:2), in which a person now lives his or her life according to the spirit of Christ that dwells in the person.

Now it is possible for this person, who once was capable only of the deeds we have already mentioned, to allow "love, joy, peace, patience, kindness, goodness, faithfulness, gentleness, self-control" to spring forth from his or her life (Galatians 5:22–23). Such a radical alteration comes from embracing the person and work of Christ and allowing Him to reign and rule in one's life.

There are many of you reading this because you are battling with the concept and practice of forgiveness. You might not even care about Jesus Christ and who He is, and you might even be offended with what has been said here. However, it would be a travesty to speak about this topic without beginning here.

The author and sustainer of life is the only one with the right to declare the truth about forgiveness. To set forth a true knowledge of forgiveness on the basis of intuition, psychological theory, or definitions and opinions of other men would only leave us in a maze of speculation without objective correctness and the idea that we have the power to do this if we just *try harder*. Only the factual proclamation of a written disclosure from the sovereign ruler of the universe can be accepted and received.

I cannot understand, comprehend, or practice forgiveness unless I begin here. There is a basic evil in every one of us. This inward corruption keeps us from the accurate knowledge and performance of forgiveness. Something must happen. It is so radical that the picture is one of cutting our heart out and replacing it with a new one. Along with this new heart must come the spirit of Christ, His very person living inside us. It is then and only then that receiving and giving mercy can become a part of our everyday living. It is a supernatural work that produces a supernatural act flowing from us. We cannot forgive on our own. Sometimes we might think we have forgiven someone, when in reality we have not. It is sobering to grasp that instead of patting ourselves on the back, we should be weeping over the fact that we do not know what it is to show others that we feel no malice toward them. May the Lord God have mercy on us for not having mercy on others. Pray this for me, and I shall pray it for you.

Chapter 2

The Experience of Forgiveness

All people like a good story. In fact, it is very difficult to keep the attention of those who live in the twenty-first century without stories, illustrations, and sensory pictures. So I want to turn your attention to a story. Now the reference here is not a story in its classical sense—a tale, an account of an imaginary event—but to a historical record. What is in mind here is the biblical account of the God-Man, Jesus Christ. The premise here is that a man or a woman who is living from an inward corruption cannot fathom the meaning of forgiveness. However, Christ came for the very purpose of forgiving us, to show us what it is and to indwell us to enable us to do the same.

This historical record begins all the way back in the third chapter of Genesis. We are confronted with our first parents: Adam and Eve. They are living in innocence, and they are enticed by the serpent, who represents Satan, to question God's word and His character. They disobey. Mankind falls from fellowship with God and a true knowledge of God. At this point, God not only shows how the restoration of this relationship will take place

(Genesis 3:15), but also His own manifestation of forgiveness is revealed when He makes clothing for the very ones who have so thanklessly ignored Him. It is God alone who has the power to forgive. Right here, in this account of Adam and Eve, we are given the understanding that individuals, because of this plunge into living apart from God, cannot in such a state genuinely forgive.

Everything else that takes place in this factual account that God gives to us is an unfolding epic leading up toward the fulfillment of that promise that God makes in Genesis 15. God deals with His people in the Old Testament through the means of a sacrificial system. All the time, He is reminding them that their greatest need is forgiveness in the midst of their disobedience. They must sacrifice repeatedly. Without the shedding of blood, there is no forgiveness. Forgiveness comes with a price. The sacrifices they make must be repeated because they are less than perfect and the blood of animals is not sufficient to remove the guilt that is real and present. Yet forgiveness is necessary; it is paramount to restoring the relationship between an individual and a holy God. God knows this. He understands the difficulty so much that God the Father chooses to send God the Son into the world to become the supreme sacrifice. The Son willingly, voluntarily, gives up His glory—His presence with the Father and the Spirit—to come and submit Himself to the limitations of manhood to bring forgiveness to those who are committed to a life of rebellion and disobedience.

Let's remind ourselves, by using another translation, who Christ came to forgive.

> They didn't bother to acknowledge God. God quit bothering them and let them run loose. And then all hell broke loose: rampant evil, grabbing and grasping, vicious backstabbing. They made life hell on earth with

their envy, wanton killing, bickering, and cheating. Look at them: mean-spirited, venomous, fork-tongued God bashers. Bullies, swaggers, insufferable windbags! They keep inventing new ways of wrecking lives. They ditch their parents when they get in the way. Slimy, cruel, coldblooded. And it's not as if they don't know better. They know perfectly well they're spitting in God's face. And they don't care—worse they hand out prizes to those who do the worse things best.

Romans 1:28–32, The Message

This is whom Jesus came to forgive. It is you and I He came to forgive. Yet to do this, He first must live a perfect life. Then He is rejected by His own followers; tried and found guilty, even though He is innocent; beaten; spit upon; mocked; nailed to a cross; and crucified. He actually takes our place on the cross and dies the death that we should die. This is the penalty for disobedience: death. He is separated from His Father for three days. He is raised from the dead. He ascends into heaven. All of this, so that forgiveness and life might be ours. This is why this has been called *The Greatest Story Ever Told*. It is just that! It is the story of forgiveness. Do we deserve such forgiveness? No! Can we earn such forgiveness? No! If you must see this story in graphic detail, rent *The Passion of the Christ* by Mel Gibson. Regardless of what you think about Mel Gibson, what he shows on the screen is a hint of the reality of Christ's death on the cross.

Or think about what happened to a tribe in the jungles of East Africa when missionaries showed them the *Jesus* film. These people had never heard of Jesus Christ, and they had never seen a motion picture. Imagine what it would feel like to see this good man, Jesus, who healed the sick and was adored by children, held without trial and beaten by jeering soldiers. As these African tribal people watched this, they became overwhelmed. They got up, standing before the screen on which the picture was displayed and shouted at the cruelty of those beating, spitting upon, and mocking Christ, demanding that this would stop. Of course, nothing happened. So they began to scream at the missionary running the projector. Since he was the one behind the picture, he could stop this. The missionary stopped the film and explained that the story wasn't over yet. Calming down, they sat back on the ground and watched with bated breath.

Next came the crucifixion. As they saw the nails being pounded into Christ's hand and feet, they began to weep and wail in such a manner that the film was stopped. The missionary attempted to calm them and again assured them that the story was not over yet. There was more to come.

Then came the resurrection. At this, an uncontrollable noise of jubilation broke out. It was deafening. The people were dancing and clapping. Christ is risen indeed! *(Nelson's Complete Book of Stories, Illustrations, and Quotes* by Robert J. Morgan.)

Everything that should happen—in the story and in their lives—is happening. This is to be happening in our own lives! There is to be a realization that everything necessary for our deliverance and forgiveness has taken place in Christ Jesus. All the blackness of our hearts and lives has been answered. Everything we have ever said, thought, or done—everything we will ever say, think, or do—has been taken away, removed, covered in the blood of Christ. We should be jumping up and down, clapping our hands, and shouting to the heavens, "Christ is risen! I am forgiven! Glory to God! Praise the name of Christ! Eternal hallelujahs! Unbelievable! No way! Impossible! Incredible! My life, my all to Christ! No reservations! Whatever you want, Lord, I will do! I am yours! Nothing do I withhold!"

We must experience this forgiveness in Christ and from Christ before we can ever know what true forgiveness is and be able to gift another person with it. It is this perfect, complete, and undeserved forgiveness that is to consume my perspective and my understanding of forgiveness—what it is, what it looks like, and how and when we should dispense it to others.

Jesus gives us a parable on forgiveness in Matthew 18. It is revealing the very same thing that we are saying here. There is a King. This King is going to settle accounts with His subjects, His slaves. There is one slave who owes the King—putting it in modern terms—ten million dollars. The King requires the slave to be sold along with his family and all his possessions. Of course, repayment would take the rest of his natural born life and then some. The point is he could never pay this debt back and he would never be in the King's presence or under His protection ever again. The slave begs the King to have patience with him and that he would repay the King everything. (We are so prideful that we think we can do whatever is required of us to make things right with a holy God when we have no concept of what we really owe.) How does the King respond? "And the lord of that slave felt compassion and released him and forgave him the debt" (v. 27). The King loves his slave. This love prompts the King to forgive His slave. There is nothing in the slave that prompts this love; there is nothing that the slave could do, because his debt is too great to earn this love. However, this great compassion produces the forgiveness.

Now this slave goes out and hunts down a fellow slave who owes him one hundred dollars. Notice the contrast here. Jesus intentionally does this. What we think someone owes us because of an offense or wrong suffered can never be compared to what we owe the One and Only True and Living God. What does this slave do? Well, he grabs hold of the one who has wronged him and chokes him while demanding him to pay the one hundred dollars (v. 28). The slave who owes the money makes the same plea that the other slave has made to the king (v. 29). The slave, who has been pardoned by the king, throws his fellow slave into prison until he pays the hundred dollars. He makes him pay. Isn't this what we do? We make people pay!

It is here that Jesus brings us to the place of looking at forgiveness through forgiveness. The King finds out and calls for this slave, who is now designated in this narrative as a "wicked slave" (v. 32) [Forgiveness received then not in turn given to someone else is labeled "wickedness."]. The King reminds this slave that he has been forgiven a huge debt. It is because he has been forgiven that he should forgive his fellow slave "in the same way that I (the King) had mercy on you." Actually, it is put in a question form. It is one of those questions that can only be answered, "Yes, of course, it only makes sense."

If the King, God Himself, has forgiven me, should I not also forgive you? YES! OF COURSE! IT ONLY MAKES SENSE! IT'S ONLY RIGHT!

Chapter 3

The Definition and Origin of Forgiveness

It must be said that practicing forgiveness is not easy. Also, it is something that we are constantly working at perfecting, knowing that we are never doing it perfectly. We must, at all times, be drawing upon the Spirit of Christ indwelling us if we have embraced Christ as our Lord and Savior, to give us the power and ability to extend mercy to those who have hurt, harmed, or wounded us or those that we love. I am not going to be able to extend forgiveness to someone unless I know and understand what it is.

"Yes, I will forgive you if you do the following things." "Yes, I will forgive you, but don't ever do it again." "Yes, I will forgive you, but you must ask for forgiveness with these words." "Yes, I will forgive you, but I will never forget what you have done." "Yes, I will forgive you, eventually, but not now." "Yes, I will forgive you, but I will always remember what you did." These attitudes and variations of them declare how most of us forgive others. It rests on the performance of other people. It is conditional. "I will forgive you, but you must do something to get it." "I will not forgive you as a gift. You have to earn it."

The problem with this is we forget that our forgiveness, to be true forgiveness, must follow the pattern of God's forgiveness for us. We are told in Colossians 3, "And so, as those who have been chosen of God, holy and beloved, put on a heart of compassion, kindness, humility, gentleness and patience; bearing with one another, and forgiving each other, whoever has a complaint against anyone; just as the Lord forgave you, so also should you [emphasis mine]" (vv. 12, 13). When we read this, our question should immediately be, "Did we do anything to earn or deserve Christ's forgiveness?" Of course, the answer is no! Christ gives His forgiveness freely. It is His grace and mercy that offer it to us. He went to the cross voluntarily to secure our pardon.

If we are to really forgive others, then we are to do it freely. Our forgiveness is not to be bought by acting a certain way or completing a certain action. Forgiveness is to be given immediately and freely. We are to set aside the offense in the same way Christ has set aside our offenses. It is to lay it aside and never pick it up again.

So here is how we will define forgiveness: *Forgiveness is the supernatural work of God's Spirit causing a person to choose to courageously set aside a wrong suffered, given freely and humbly, having been overwhelmed by the forgiveness one has received through the cross of Christ and done solely for Christ's glory and honor, no matter what has been done or who has done it.*

Let us say here that this definition cannot be divorced from what we have already said. Everything connected to true forgiveness has to be seen in light of what we have already seen in regard to the person and work of Christ. You and I do not have the ability, in our fallen nature, to forgive anybody. The very core of our hearts and lives must first be radically changed. Then and only then can we draw upon a power source deep inside that enables us to look at someone who has terribly wounded us and say, "I forgive you!"

It is very important that we understand that we are not talking about a "feeling," a warm, fuzzy, tingly emotion that fosters an attitude of pity. We do not wait until we experience a sensation of sympathy, empathy, or compassion for another person. Actually, our emotions, in the proper giving of forgiveness, are directed toward the great Lover of our souls. We are bound to the One who has been slain and who has shed His blood on our behalf. Our forgiveness of another person is initially not even for his or her sake. We forgive for the purpose of demonstrating our love for our great Lord and Savior, Jesus Christ. We forgive because we love Christ. We forgive to please Him. We forgive out of obedience to His will. We forgive because it is what He wants us to do.

In that great passage of instruction to His disciples on how they should pray, Jesus says that one of the most important aspects of praying is to seek forgiveness for their sins. The interesting thing is that their forgiveness rests on the fact that they have forgiven those who have done something against them: "And forgive us our debts, as we also have forgiven our debtors" (Matthew 6:12). Then at the end of this model prayer that the disciples are instructed to use, Jesus gives them a short commentary on this whole subject of forgiveness: "For if you forgive men for their transgressions, your heavenly Father will also forgive you. But if you do not forgive men, then your Father will not forgive your transgressions" (Matthew 6:14, 15). What? Did we hear what Jesus is saying? If we do not forgive someone who has done something against us and we think they owe us something because of it (a "debt"), or that they have overstepped their bounds in their dealings with us (a "transgression"), then God is not obligated to forgive us.

Our forgiveness is bound to our forgiving. Of course, this cannot be in reference to our initial forgiveness and coming into a saving relationship with Christ. There are no works involved in our being justified before God on the basis of the perfect work of Christ. However, this must be in reference to our daily living, our sanctification; it must be evidence of our genuine relationship with Christ. If I do not forgive others, I am not forgiven, which declares that I was never forgiven in the first place. Now I am sure some of you will not like this line of reasoning, but it appears to be the only conclusion we can come to. Jesus is serious about forgiveness and our forgiving others. It is not an option. It is something that determines our eternal relationship with Christ. If we are truly His, we will forgive.

It would again seem, from the Lord's Prayer, that forgiveness is something I do and not something I feel. Our obedience declares our love for Christ. Jesus says, "If you love Me you will keep my commandments" (John 14:15). We act on His will and forgive others not because we feel a certain way toward them but because "the love of Christ controls us, having concluded this [we think a certain way], that one died for all, therefore all died [my hatred, my bitterness, my anger, my feelings of abandonment, betrayal, woundedness, hurt, etc.]; and He died for all, that they who live should no longer live for themselves, but for Him who died and rose again on their behalf" [brackets mine] (2 Corinthians 5:14, 15).

Do we understand this? My fear is that we do not. Yet this is how we are to see this whole subject of forgiveness. We must do what we are instructed to do: "And do not be conformed to this world, but be transformed by the *renewing of your mind*, that you may prove what the will of God is, that which is good and acceptable and perfect" [emphasis mine] (Romans 12:2). *Don't feel! Think!* We must think about our lives, our responses to people and to circumstances from God's great and glorious perspective, His mind-set and not ours. You and I do not deserve to be forgiven. We only deserve God's wrath and condemnation. Amazingly, He freely forgives us—completely, unconditionally, perfectly! Now our response to others is to forgive them. It doesn't matter how deep the hurt is. Do we love Jesus? Then you and I have no choice.

Let's put ourselves in a practical situation. I come to your door and knock. When you open the door, what do you see? You see the person who has fired you for no apparent reason, who has destroyed your reputation by spreading lies and rumors, who divorced you and wrecked your life, who slept with your spouse, who was drunk and killed your teenage son or daughter, who raped your daughter, or who _____
(fill in the blank). I am there to ask you to forgive me. What do you do?

It might be good to stress here what we don't do. We do not decide whether the person that is asking for forgiveness is sincere or not. We do not make a judicial decision concerning the degree of repentance shown by the one asking us to forgive him or her. These are things that only the Judge of all the earth knows. We have not been given the responsibility of reading the hearts of people. Nothing in the biblical passages that we have referred to on forgiveness has said anything about the forgiver determining the sincerity of the one seeking pardon. All the passages refer to the state of the heart and the action of the forgiver. In fact, even if the person never shows up at our door, we are, before the Lord of glory, responsible to forgive that person without a word proceeding from his or her mouth or an indication of repentance on his or her part. Hard? Difficult? Impossible? You bet! That is, if we are going to depend on ourselves. Remember the definition we began with in this chapter says that it is a "supernatural work of God's Spirit." We can't do it! Only God can do it through us.

Back to the question, "What do we do?" As we look at that person, or visualize that person, we begin to think about who we are in Christ Jesus. We consciously, in our minds, put on the very robe of righteousness that Christ has given to us. We, because of the cross and His shed blood, become blood-bought covenant sons and daughters. We possess the very attitude of Christ that caused Him to humble Himself and take on "the form of a bond-servant" and be made "in the likeness of men" and "humbled Himself by becoming obedient to the point of death, even death on a cross" (Philippians 2:5–8). As our garment, we put on "the peace of Christ," we put on "the word of Christ," and we put on the love of Christ (Colossians 3:12–17). We put on "a heart of compassion, kindness, humility, gentleness and patience" (Colossians 3:12). We actually become this "new creature" or "new creation" in Christ Jesus (2 Corinthians 5:17).

Clark Kent puts on his suit and becomes Superman, Bruce Wayne puts on his suit and becomes Batman, and Peter Parker puts on his suit and becomes Spider-Man. This is what happens to the person who opens the door. They are now clothed in the light of Jesus Christ. They are living in a new sphere, a new realm that causes them to look at the person on the other side of the door and say, "Yes, I forgive you!" It is a powerful and glorious statement of the reality of who we have become in Christ Jesus.

This is what forgiveness is. It flows from one who knows beyond question that he has been forgiven. His forgiveness compels him to forgive. It is not how he feels that determines his actions. It is the unquestionable love of Christ for him that has set him free and washed away all his iniquity and wickedness past, present, and future. The understanding and experience of such unimaginable love constrains his heart and he knows he must forgive. He will forgive! It is now part of his new makeup. It pours out of his life.

Chapter 4

The Characteristics of True Forgiveness

In trying to think how to begin this chapter, I thought, *What is one of the greatest modern accounts of true forgiveness?* The answer came from a very unlikely source: *Spider-Man 3*. That's right! I am not sure who came up with this storyline, but throughout this movie one is confronted with the struggle that plagues every person in the area of holding anger and bitterness in the core of one's being.

Peter Parker, aka Spider-Man, is consumed with his anger and bitterness toward the one who killed Uncle Ben, the man who raised him like a father. The killer has escaped prison and, due to some kind of chemical reaction, has become the Sandman. His whole body is made of sand that allows him to take shapes and forms and become a great, powerful, menacing, force. Peter's rage and hatred attract a "symbiotic alien," that is represented by this black goo that covers his body while he is lying in bed. It literally turns his suit black. It covers him. It binds itself to him. It does not just cover the outside, but it covers Peter on the inside too. It causes the evil in Peter Parker to come alive.

When Spider-Man faces the "Sandman," in his black suit, his only aim is to destroy him. He thinks he has. When Aunt Mae asks him what happened, Peter nonchalantly says, "Spider-Man killed him." In disbelief, Aunt Mae responds, "Spider-Man doesn't kill people! What happened?" Peter has no answer. Something similar happens as Peter is talking with his girlfriend, MJ. She sees that something has terribly gone wrong in the character of this man she has come to love. At one critical point, MJ says, "Who are you?" Peter's response: "I don't know!"

As Peter struggles with all of this, in one of the great symbolic scenes in the movie, Peter walks out into the rain after speaking with MJ. He looks up and sees a cross on the top of a church steeple. He goes into the church and there he commences to tear from his body the symbiotic alien. He yells and screams in the midst of the great pain and agony that this removal causes him.

The next encounter Peter has with the Sandman is radically different from the first. Peter is now in his red and blue Spider-Man suit, the one that represents the hero and all the good that dwells in him. The Sandman tells Peter the situation that he was in when his gun accidently went off and killed Uncle Ben. The Sandman says, "I am not asking you to forgive me. I just want you to understand." Peter's response is—*listen carefully*—this: "I've done terrible things too." Sandman says, "The only thing left to me now is my daughter." Then the great pronouncement comes from the lips of our hero: "I forgive you."

Now this is not the only panorama of forgiveness that is given to us in this movie. There is Peter and MJ. There is Peter and Harry. Over and over again, we are confronted with the need for forgiveness to produce peace, restore friendship, mend broken lives, and do a host of other things that only forgiveness can produce.

I present this initial picture as a stepping off place for us to consider together the essential qualities of true forgiveness. However, before we do that, I will take a moment to remind us of our great problem. Just like Peter, we have been overtaken by a symbiotic alien, a sinful nature, that controls us unless we have come to the place of giving ourselves over to One who can strip it from us and implant within us a new heart that makes us new creatures in Christ. Of course, this is why even movies fall short of the true picture of human beings and their real condition. Whereas Peter Parker is shown as having the ability to rip off his other self, it is very clear, from God's perspective, that you and I do not have the power to perform that inhuman feat on our own. God in all of His power and glory must do that for us.

C. S. Lewis pictures it best in *The Voyage of the Dawn Treader*. A boy named Eustace is one of the main characters in this classic tale. Eustace is selfish, greedy, and mean-spirited. He turns into a dragon that depicts the very nature he has exemplified: a cold-blooded monster. Only when he sees himself for who he really is—an unpleasant, self-centered person—does he want to be human again. "He wanted to get back among humans and talk and laugh and share things. He realized he was a monster cut off from the whole human race. An appalling loneliness came over him" (chapter 6, paragraphs 34–35).

Coming to grips with this, Eustace is determined to get out of his dragon skin. He tries to do it himself, but he can't. Then Aslan, the great lion who is Lewis' representation of Christ, comes to Eustace and the narrative tells us this: "Then the lion said—but I don't know if it spoke—'You will have to let me undress you.'

I was afraid of his claws; I can tell you, but I was pretty nearly desperate now. So I just lay flat down on my back to let him do it. The very first tear he made was so deep and I thought it had gone right into my heart. And when he began pulling the skin off, it hurt worse than anything I've ever felt" (chapter 7, paragraphs 41–42). Yes, the great God of this universe must remove that which causes us to selfishly live our lives and to lash out at those around us who we feel are violating our privileges.

This brings us then to the elements, or what we are calling the characteristics, of true forgiveness. As we go through these, we need to say upfront that these are by no means exhaustive or are they put in any order of importance. They are, I believe, necessary, and all must be present to manifest a forgiveness to others that sets them and us free.

A Choice, Not a Feeling

Spider-Man, at the end of the movie, is speaking about the whole subject of forgiveness. This is what he says: "Whatever comes our way. Whatever battle is raging inside of us, we always have a choice. It is the choices that make us who we are; and we can always choose what is right." Great insight! Some of what he says is true; other things are false. Yes, a choice must be made and the choice reveals who we are. The problem is we do not have the power in and of ourselves to make the right choice—as one completely under the power of the symbiotic alien, Spider-Man could not do what was right—and, therefore, we do not always do what is right. Again, we have already laid the groundwork for us to understand that we must draw upon the power of the Spirit of God to make right choices.

The point is that when we think about forgiveness, we must tell ourselves, until it becomes engrained in our very souls, that our forgiveness of another person must have nothing to do with how we feel toward him or her. Forgiveness is a matter of the will, not of emotions. Remember the "wicked slave" we talked about? It says that "he was *unwilling*" (emphasis mine) to forgive his fellow slave (Matthew 18:30). Forgiveness is something I must choose to do. It is based on my confident trust in the fact that this is what my heavenly Father has commanded me to do. There are no exceptions to this, and to demonstrate my love for Him and my established purpose to please Him, I do it!

Okay, I am going to go to a place I probably shouldn't. I will probably make a lot of people upset, my children included. However, I do this because I am convinced that we no longer *think* the way God wants us to think. My emphasis here is on thinking, which determines what I choose. So much of our living today, even among those who profess to be Christians, is directed by modern-day psychology, psychoanalysis, psychiatry, and even personality systems that tell us all we need is self-understanding, insight into ourselves, which brings about correction in a person's life. It is this understanding that leads to self-actualization, which will then lead to self-esteem. In fact, it has become more and more difficult, if not wrong, to talk to people about what God's Word says in light of their wanting to talk about their family history and what their parents have done to them or the ways in which they have learned to cope with issues in their lives. Everyone is dysfunctional and everyone has a past that keeps him or her from being able to make decisions and go through life having a clear vision of who he or she is and how he or she is to live. The basic question is always this: "How do you feel?" It is no longer this: "What does God say? What do you think?"

It appears that we are consumed with the concept of feelings. We want to know how a person feels because we want to get behind the feeling to the cause. We want people to feel better about themselves so that they can get by better in the world that is pressing in around them. This is a classical man-centered approach to the inner heart and life of individuals. So often, even Christian psychologists, who are caught up in an integrationist perspective of blending a particular school or theory of psychology with Christian values, approach their counseling from this humanistic frame of mind. Many actually give credence to what they are doing by using the phrase "all truth is God's truth." This is certainly so, only if the truth they are setting forth about man and who he is coincides with God "true truth," as revealed in His Word.

Christian counselors are often content with trying to help people "cope" (which itself is not a biblical concept) with the life they are living. The Word of God says nothing about "coping" or "looking out for oneself," "surviving," "carrying on," or handling" or "managing" life. It talks about "fighting," "wrestling," "doing battle," "putting to death," "mastering it," and always referring to the concept of "sin" in our lives. In the most powerful and descriptive way, it says, "For though we walk in the flesh we do not war according to the flesh *(This cannot be a man-centered life. I have no hope if it is. As much as knowing my past might help, it will never get me through this life.)*, for the weapons of our warfare are not of the flesh, but divinely powerful for the destruction of fortresses. We are *destroying* speculations and every lofty thing raised up against the *knowledge of God*, and we are taking every *thought* captive to the obedience of Christ" [emphasis mine] (2 Corinthians 10:3–5). There is nothing here about asking, "How do you feel?" It is all about, "What do you know? What are you going to do?"

If we believe that helping people cope gives them truth, we are not giving them God-centered truth. We may be giving them partial truth or half-truth, but really, ultimately, that is a lie. People must know that they have a black, symbiotic alien attached to their souls, and unless they allow the infinite, personal, God to strip it from them, they are doomed in this world and the next. They are called to do battle with all that would keep them from demonstrating their love for the One who came to die for them. Every man, woman, and child must know this. This is what Christ has commanded us to do in the Great Commission. It doesn't matter whether the person we are talking to professes to be a Christian or not. We are under the command of our King. We cannot do anything less; and anything that falls short of this is false.

The point? My father may have raped me, my parents or husband may have abandoned me, my spouse may have betrayed me, someone may have killed my loved one, or my employer may have fired me. But, barring chemical imbalance, being mentally incapable, having been diagnosed as schizophrenic, or having other true mental problems, we must know who God has revealed Himself to be. We must know what He has done for us and that, as one who belongs to Him, we take our thoughts of betrayal, abandonment, etc., to Him and in obedience choose to forgive. We must know of Christ's forgiveness in the midst of our great hurts and woundedness. Forgiveness is a work! It is something we do, not something we feel, but we must know it to be able to do it.

We must go through the mental exercise of "putting on" and "putting off." What do we put on? We have already mentioned some of this, but let's do it again. We strip off those things, those feelings, that would keep us from forgiving and put on the bloodstained robe of righteousness that Christ has given to us—His righteousness. It would also be helpful at this point to mention that great passage in Ephesians 6. Every day we are to become this warrior who is going out to battle, who knows that he or she cannot face the terrors and trials of this life or be victorious without the armor of God.

This passage bears quoting in its entirety. Read it carefully. Understand that as you and I walk through this life, we are in desperate need of each of these pieces. Here it is:

> Finally, be strong in the Lord and in the strength of His might. Put on the full armor of God, so that you will be able to stand firm against the schemes of the Devil. For our struggle is not against flesh and blood, but against the rulers, against the powers, against the world forces of wickedness in the heavenly places. Therefore, take up the full armor of God, so that you will be able to resist in the evil day, and having done everything, to stand firm. Stand firm therefore, HAVING GIRDED YOUR LOINS WITH TRUTH, AND HAVING PUT ON THE BREASTPLATE OF RIGHTEOUSNESS, and having shod YOUR FEET WITH THE PREPARATION OF THE GOSPEL OF PEACE; in addition to all, taking up the shield of faith with which you will be able to extinguish all the flaming arrows of the evil one. And take THE HELMET OF SALVATION, and the sword of the Spirit, which is the word of God. With all prayer and petition, pray at all times in the Spirit ...
>
> Ephesians 6:10–18a

In quoting this, I am reminded of how often I live without the reality of the truth of this passage gripping my heart and life. Consciously, we need to clothe ourselves each day. Don't think that you or I can choose to forgive someone on our own. Why do we need to do this? Look again at those words in verse 16: "You will be able to extinguish all the flaming arrows of the evil one." Beloved, do not think that you are just flying through life without a care in the world. There are unseen forces that seek to destroy us. You think you can forgive someone in your own strength and power? Don't be naïve. Enemies are planning how to stop you. Temptations are crouching at your door to keep you from showing compassion and love to those around you. The world, the Devil, and your own flesh are calibrated to fill your heart and mine with hatred, bitterness, resentment, revenge, and everything that would block our desire and ability to extend forgiveness to those around us.

A Setting Aside/A Putting On

In Psalm 103:11–12, we are told what the LORD, the sovereign God of the universe, has done with our "transgressions" (rebellion against godly living). It says, "As far as the east is from the west, so far has He removed our transgressions from us." The prophet Nathan, in light of confronting David with reference to his sins of adultery and murder, and David's acknowledgment of his wrong doing, says, "The LORD also has taken away your sin; you shall not die" (2 Samuel 12:13). Isaiah declares that the LORD has "cast all my sins behind Your back" (38:17), and again that He is the one who "wipes out our transgressions" (43:25). The prophet Zechariah tells us that God "will remove the iniquity of the land" (3:9). The author of Hebrews reveals that Christ has borne our sins and has been "manifested to put away sin by the sacrifice of Himself" (9:26).

The phrases that are prominent in each of the above quoted verses are "removed our transgressions," "taken away your sin," "cast all my sins behind Your back," "wipes out our transgressions," "will

DR. GEORGE W. MITCHELL

remove," and "put away sin." We see here that in dealing with our sins, which enables forgiveness to be accomplished, God takes action against them. He does something with them. We should take notice here that nothing is said in regard to "forgetting" sin. It is actively removing them, putting them aside. The will is exercised in dealing with sin, not the feelings. In the case of our sovereign God, a work, a righteousness that is not ours, intervenes and the blood of Christ wipes them away. We are clothed in that righteousness. The garment of sin that we have been wearing is ripped off us and replaced with Christ's garment. Forgiveness is ours on the basis of this garment.

In the same way, because we are the redeemed and are sons and daughters of our great King, we realize that if we are to forgive anyone, we must set aside their wrongdoing toward us—and what it tends to produce in us. We take the anger, the bitterness, the hurt, the resentment, the hatred, the jealousy, and the pride and consciously lay it aside. We toss it, as it were, into the deepest pit that we can conceive. We remove it, we take it away, we cast it off, and we put it away. We do with it what we know the God of all creation has done with ours.

This, however, is not done by itself. At the same time we set something aside, we must put something on. We have already alluded to this. When we take a garment off and put it aside, if we remain without covering, we lay ourselves open to the elements, and in many cases those very things that we put off will come flooding back into our hearts and lives fourfold, making those feelings of hurt greater than they were before. This is why we are given the picture in Scripture that we are to "put on a heart of compassion, kindness, humility, gentleness and patience; bearing with one another, and forgiving each other, whoever has a complaint against anyone …" (Colossians 3:12, 13). We are to let "all bitterness and wrath and anger and clamor and slander be put away from you, along with all malice; and be kind to one another, tender-hearted forgiving each other just as God in Christ also has forgiven you" (Ephesians 4:31, 32). Setting aside and putting on, putting on and putting away—this is to be our practice.

Is this easy? Can we do this? No! We cannot do this by our own will power. We cannot grunt enough, exert ourselves enough, to cause this to happen. We cannot just try harder. We need a power source that is outside our sinful, fallen selves. You will never forgive me! I will never forgive you! We are so self-centered, so self-consumed, that it is impossible in and of ourselves to do something so radical. That is why, if we are in Christ, if the grace of God has captured our very souls, we have been given the Holy Spirit, the same power that raised Jesus Christ from the dead. The Spirit is living within us to give us God's enabling grace to accomplish all that we have been commanded to do. We are to call upon the Holy Spirit to help us to die to our own selfish desires to punish other people for what they have done and, instead, love them as Christ has commanded us to love them.

We are to cry out to God for His supernatural power. Listen, we are not talking here about the sloppy, anemic, heartless, insincere, type of praying that most of us are used to. We need to be serious about great need in our lives to forgive others. The writer of Hebrews, in talking about fighting sin in our lives, and unforgiveness is sin, says, "You have not yet resisted to the point of shedding blood in striving against sin" (Hebrews 12:4). Do we know anything about this kind of praying: "shedding blood in our striving against sin"?

We can't forgive somebody on our own? What do we do? Have we literally prostrated ourselves on the floor before the living God and cried out, "Oh, God! Oh, God! Help me! I am overcome by the blackness of my own heart. I hate! I hate this person! Take this terrible wickedness and iniquity out of my heart! I literally desire to do harm to someone else. You have commanded me to love even my enemies in the very same way You have loved me. And yet, all I know right now is deep anger, resentment, bitterness, and murder in my heart. Take all of this from me. Give me the power to lay it aside. Do not let me rise from the floor until I know that Your Spirit has given me the grace to put it away. Let me put on Your compassion, love, patience, gentleness, goodness, self-control. Let me extend complete and full forgiveness to this person. Have mercy upon me! Oh, Lord, forgive me for every wrong desire and feeling in my heart. Cleanse me with the blood of Christ! Let me know Your love for me. Let the resurrected life of Jesus Christ reign in my life."

We keep praying in this way until, if need be, we are shedding those drops of blood.

This is serious business. This is no game! We are told in Hebrews 12:14, "Pursue peace with all men, and the sanctification without which no one will see the Lord." It is not just forgiveness, but we are to be "at peace" with all men. It is our responsibility to be "peacemakers," as Christ Himself reminds us in the Beatitudes (Matthew 5:9). It is important to understand that our relationships are to be free of that state in which we would hold something against someone else and cause division and dissention. Remembering, at the same time, that we have already seen that if we do not forgive, God says He has the right to declare that we are not His. This goes back to the Lord's Prayer. If we are not forgiven, then the implication is that we do not know God's forgiveness and are still in our sins. This is something we must do. It is so important that God has given us His Spirit to actually enable us to accomplish this great work.

An Action Not Based on Motive or
Outward Behavior of Another Person

CSI Miami is not necessarily the greatest teacher of accurate thinking or accurate actions. Yet, like anything else, sometimes the show does get it right. In one of its episodes, a lady has everything wrong and is constantly attacking Horatio and what he is doing to try to bring the perpetrator to justice. At the end, of course, our hero is right and has done everything, in the midst of constantly being challenged and accused of wrongdoing, to demonstrate a kind and caring attitude toward this individual who has been so obnoxious. The final scene shows the woman coming up to Horatio, as he is leaning over a rail in a very relaxed position, and acknowledging (not in these exact words, but close), "I am sorry for doubting you and for treating you the way that I have. Will you forgive me?" Horatio's response is (these are the exact words): "Already done!"

It is important to understand that in the process of our forgiving another person, our primary concern focuses on what God expects us to do. So often, our forgiveness is conditioned on the response or behavior of the other person. We want to know if he or she is really sorry. Oftentimes, before we extend forgiveness, we demand that the other person recognizes what he has done and ask that we forgive him. In all of this, we are insisting that our forgiveness is tied to the other person's repentance or lack of it.

We need to return to Romans 12. It is here that we are instructed that our transformation is based on the "renewing of your mind" (v. 2). The world bases its forgiveness (which can never be true forgiveness) on whether a person is responding properly to what he has done against another. We, as those who are "in Christ," do not want "to be conformed to this world" (v. 2). This is why we do not forgive on the basis of feelings bound up in whether people are responding in the way we feel they should. No! Our position is that we respond on the basis of what we know (knowledge truth, how we think) God has said and what He has done in forgiving us. Our forgiveness, as we have pointed out in more than one place, is to conform to the forgiveness that has been given to us in Christ. Christ does not forgive us because we deserve it or because our repentance is perfect. He forgives us freely because we need it to be made right with a holy God.

Our forgiveness, then, is not because someone has met a certain requirement or deserves it but because we are commanded to do so—not only for the sake of the one forgiven but for our own sake to demonstrate our conformity to the very image of Christ. We are to act like Christ. We are to mirror His character in all things. His glory, not our retribution or our gauge as to whether a person is really sorry for what he has done, is to be the determining factor in our forgiveness.

Another person's lack of repentance, selfish motives, continued purpose to do what is wrong, or general indifference is to mean nothing to us. We are not directed in what we do by him or her. Our allegiance is to the King of Glory, and it should be our desire and design to please Him. What will please Him and forever establish His kingdom is that the name of Christ and in the likeness of Christ we extend forgiveness to those who need it without any thought of whether they deserve it. Christ lives in us. Hear Paul's great declaration: "I have been crucified with Christ; and it is no longer I who live, but Christ lives in me; and the life which I now live in the flesh I live by faith in the Son of God, who loved me, and delivered Himself up for me" (Galatians 2:20).

We are to live as dead men and women. My wants, my wishes, my desires, my anger, my hurt, my bitterness, my resentfulness, and my determination to hurt you back—all of this is dead. This is exactly the point of Galatians 2:20. The life we are living right now is to have nothing to do with us. We do not matter! We do not exist! It is Christ that matters. He is living His glorious life through us. We do not consider what the other person has done to us. By faith, we have our whole being riveted on how Christ will respond to that person through us. We have been crucified. We are dead to that old self that wants to stick the knife in and twist it. We are living in newness of life and abiding in, living in the realm of, Christ Jesus. Everything has changed.

A No Respecter of Persons

It doesn't matter who the person is: friend, spouse, mother, father, brother, sister, coworker, employer, employee, or our greatest enemy. All are to be given the supernatural forgiveness that comes in and through Christ. We don't really know what to do with our Lord's instruction in Luke's statement of Christ's Sermon on the Mount when Jesus says, "But I say to you who hear, love your enemies, do good to those who hate you, bless those who curse you, pray for those who mistreat you" (6:27–28). Again, in the same chapter, Christ says, "But love your enemies, and do good, and lend, expecting nothing in return; and your reward will be great, and you will be sons of the Most High; for He Himself is kind to ungrateful and evil men. Be merciful, just as your Father is merciful" (vv. 35–36). No, this is not made up. Here it is! What do we do with our enemies? We love them! We do good to them! We bless them! We pray for those who mistreat us! We lend to them while expecting nothing! We are to be merciful to them! Certainly, then, we forgive them! We do not hold anything against them. We do not treat them any less than we do our closest friend or our dearest loved one.

It is important here that when Jesus says we are to love our enemies, we fully understand the implications of His instruction. There is no greater exposition of what love really is than in 1 Corinthians 13. In summing it up, here is how we are to love our enemies: "Love is patient. Love is kind. Love is not jealous. Love does not brag and is not arrogant. Love does not act unbecomingly. Love does not seek its own. Love is not provoked. Love does not take into account a wrong suffered. Love does not rejoice in unrighteousness. Love rejoices with the truth. Love bears all things, believes all things, hopes all things, and endures all things. And love never fails" (vv. 4–8). There it is! This is what you and I are to give fully and without reservation to our enemies.

We cannot say, "They are my enemy" or "But you don't know what they have done to me or to the one who is closest to my heart." Sorry, it makes no difference. There is no excuse! There is no reason! To make it very plain, we are told why we are to do this. Why? Because our heavenly Father is "kind to ungrateful and evil men." This is what distinguishes us as belonging to the family of God. This is what makes us "sons of the Most High."

Identification! Who do we belong to? Do you and I withhold our forgiveness? Then we are not sons and daughters of the Most High. If this is not so, then the only answer is that we are sons and daughters of the Devil himself. Please, we cannot skip through our day thinking that if we are not imitating the life of Christ in our dealings and actions with others, it is not really that bad and our mistakes will be overlooked and winked at by the Holy and sovereign God of this universe. We only have the right to say, "Abba, Father," if it is the expressed longing in our lives to please Him in all things and to look like Him in the practice of our lives.

"And opening his mouth, Peter said: 'I most certainly understand now that God is not one to show partiality'" (Acts 10:34). In Romans, Paul says, "For there is no partiality with God" (Romans 2:11). "God shows no partiality ..." (Galatians 2:6). "Honor all men ..." (1 Peter 2:17). This is who God is! This is who you and I must be if we are His sons and daughters.

Not Punitive, Restricted, or Conditional

In all that has been said so far, hopefully this characteristic of forgiveness should be quite evident. Forgiveness, to be real forgiveness, is not given in any way that causes the person guilty of an offense to believe that forgiveness is not genuine. If forgiveness is based on our performance, and we are the recipients of forgiveness, we will never know if our performance is satisfactory or not. We are fallen people, sinners, and it is our failure to perform in the first place that brought about our wrong behavior. A person who knows the free and perfect forgiveness of Christ in his or her own life knows how powerful and freeing it is to have one's sin set aside without any conditions attached. In the case of our forgiveness in Christ, we have additionally been clothed with the garments of perfect righteousness and the ability to put on compassion, patience, gentleness, and humility. How utterly glorious and wonderful this is. Knowing this, we come offering forgiveness, not to continue the slavery of another caught up in his offense but to release him. At the same time, we are set free.

In that great little devotional *Steams in the Desert: 1*, we are given a great picture that is recorded on June 22. It recounts a deep struggle that "a precious child of God" is having one sleepless night as a "cruel injustice" sweeps over her. As she talks about this, she refers to "the love which covers seemed to have crept out of my heart." Her reference here is Proverbs 10:12b: "But love

37

covers all transgressions" (remembering we are commanded by Jesus to even love our enemies). This beloved saint continues by saying, "Then I cried to God in an agony for the power to obey His instruction, 'Love covereth.'" Now listen to the rest of what she declares: "Mentally I dug a grave. Deliberately I threw up the earth until the excavation was deep. Sorrowfully I lowered into it the thing which wounded me. Quickly I shoveled in the clods. Over the mouth, I carefully laid the green sods. Then I covered it with white roses and forget-me-nots and quickly walked away."

Oh, God, give me the power and the wisdom to do this! How incredibly wise! There is no condition the other person must meet. In fact, he or she was not even present. He or she was not even the "thing" that was buried. It was the thing, the injustice itself, that was covered up. This is a picture of a true setting aside. In fact, it is not just a setting aside but the digging of a deep grave to bury it in. In the place of this "cruel injustice" is put "white roses and forget-me-nots." This great saint quickly walks away. Oh, in the agony of our souls, in the blackness that would creep over our hearts, may we cry out to our God to give us His supernatural strength to dig our graves and to cast whatever it is that seeks to produce the "gall of bitterness" in us into the depths of that pit, cover it up, replace it with all that is beautiful in Christ, and walk away from it.

A Restorer of Relationships

When something has been done to us, immediately we no longer look at a person in the same way as we did before. A great gulf begins to form between us and the other person. We start erecting a wall. We lay bricks one at a time or we throw the whole wall up. This barrier between the other person and us causes us to not talk to the other person, to not want to be in the same room with him, to look at him differently (looks that are sometimes filled with all kinds of animosity), and to take the position (unconsciously or consciously) that, in light of what he has done, he is less than the person he was. Our lack of forgiveness and our waiting for that person to meet our conditions leads to great destruction. In most cases, it does not only affect us and the other person but everyone else connected to both. Whole groups of people, families, businesses, schools, offices, and churches have been decimated by those who refuse to offer forgiveness.

Our frame of reference here is from the perspective of those who have received the forgiveness that is theirs in Christ. As blood-bought men and women, forgiveness is not an option. It is that which is commanded. This forgiveness is a glorious, transforming force. It is this forgiveness that must and will restore relationships and make things right. The command to us is to "pursue peace with all men" (Hebrews 12:14). The emphasis here is one of extreme exertion on our part to bring about reconciliation. People who haven't forgiven each other are not at peace. There is actually enmity between us if we are not in a state of peace. The only thing that will break down the wall that has been built is to give pardon to those who need it from us.

Extending true forgiveness to other people restores completely the relationship that was there before the division. They are no longer second-class citizens in the realm of our relationships. We do not treat them any differently than we treat someone else who has never done anything to hurt us. We have set their offenses aside. We have dug that grave. The offenses are no longer before us. They will never, never, never be referred to again. I look at the people, and if they are believers, I speak to the Christ in them. If they are unbelievers, I speak to them as an image bearer of God with a love for them that desires they know the Savior that I know.

I say all of this knowing firsthand the looks that people give to you when they have been hurt by you. I know what it is not to be forgiven. I know what it is for people to say that they have forgiven you when in reality they have not and the wall keeping you out remains and grows even thicker. I know what it means to have sought repeatedly for someone's forgiveness and to have been refused repeatedly.

All of this continues to foster enmity, strife, and the inability to bring about the reconciliation that Christ commands. Forgiveness that is authentic and genuine reconciles people to each other. It brings a unity and oneness of heart that causes us to delight in each other's presence again and brings that peace we have been directed to pursue. If we do not experience this with those who have offended us, maybe it stems from the awful, and yet true, reality that we have never forgiven them.

An Act Born of Courage

I remember like it was yesterday being in the position of associate pastor of Christian education at Briarwood Presbyterian Church in Birmingham, Alabama, and being at a session meeting. A session meeting is a group of officers who are responsible for the spiritual oversight of the members of a particular church. There are teaching elders, those who have a special calling to the teaching ministry, and ruling elders, laymen in the church who, meeting the qualifications for their particular office, have been elected by the congregation. Briarwood is a very large church, so there were some fifty elders present that night.

One of the ruling elders stood up and criticized an aspect of ministry that happened to be under my responsibility. Now I was convinced that this fellow elder was entirely wrong in what he was saying. So, not being a shy or reserved person, I immediately stood up and spoke to this issue, making it plain how, in every point, this brother in Christ had been misinformed.

As I was driving home, God's Spirit began to poke and prod at my heart. When I got to the house, I immediately shared with my wife what had transpired. She looked at me, as only she could, and without giving me an extensive look into the intricacies of what had happened, simply said, "George, you know what you need to do." The knife of truth in regard to what she said went in and cut deep into my soul where the Lord and I were most intimate. I knew that what I said was true, but the way I said it was wrong.

The next day, I went to the person in charge of setting up the agenda for the next session meeting, which, by the way, was a month away, and asked him to put me on the docket. At the next meeting, when my time came, I stood up and looked out at those fifty men. All month there had been times of apprehension that gripped my heart. Questions came to mind: "What will they think?" "How will they receive this?" "How will they think of me afterward?" Of course, I knew I couldn't just go to the man I had spoken against at the meeting, because I had said what I had said to the whole group.

I stood and said, "Gentlemen, fathers and brothers in Christ, I need to ask you to forgive me for what I said at the last session meeting. Len, I especially address this to you, but I need to ask all of you to forgive me. I need to ask you to forgive me for my lack of love and respect for all of you as I spoke. I sought to speak the truth, but I did not speak it in love and I spoke out of pride and arrogance. So will you forgive me?

Well, that is very close to what I said. It is not word for word, because it has been some years since this took place. But it is very vivid to me, because it took so much courage born of much prayer and crying out to the Lord God to help me. It is amazing to me to think about how many of those men came up to me afterward and said, "Thank you, George. No one has ever stood up in a session meeting and asked us to forgive him."

Now I know this example has to do with asking for forgiveness and not giving forgiveness. However, the truth is that both of them come from the same place. They come from the heart of a person who is deeply aware of how great his sins are. There is that realization that inside there is all manner of evil and, because of this, outside (except for the grace of God) we are capable of doing everything that is wicked and vile. This is what Jesus came to remove by His death on the cross. There is forgiveness for all of these sins, past, present, and future. This is what makes a person able to look someone else in the eyes and say either one of these difficult statements: "Will you forgive me?" or "I forgive you."

Giving forgiveness is not easy. In fact, if we really understand everything we have been saying here, it is not natural. Part of the definition that we set forth earlier states that it is a "supernatural act." This is something the living God must do in and through us. So as we are praying about forgiveness, we need to pray that the Lord God will give us the courage to do it.

We need the courage to die to self. There is no way that we can by those who identify with Christ if we do not die to ourselves. Jesus makes this very clear when He says, "If anyone wishes to come after me, let him deny himself, and take up his cross daily, and follow Me" (Luke 9:23). Death to all that we are must characterize our lives in order to even think about forgiving other people. The whole idea of an offense is that it is done to "poor me." You and I cannot think that we can even begin to be involved that most difficult task of all—forgiveness—if we are preoccupied with self.

Running a close second to this is the courage not to yield to our own desires, those deep, dark hungerings of the soul—anger, malice, bitterness, resentfulness, and the consuming urge to hurt the other person by withholding ourselves from him or her. Sound familiar? They do to me. We must hate those cravings. We must fight against them! Repent of them! Kill them! Do whatever it takes to keep them from wreaking havoc in our inner man. The writer of Hebrews tells us, "Let us also lay aside every encumbrance, and the sin which so easily entangles us, and let us run with endurance the race that is set before us, fixing our eyes on Jesus, the author and perfecter of faith, who for the joy set before Him endured the cross, despising the shame, and has set down at the right hand of the throne of God" (Hebrews 12:1–2). It is a marathon race, and our power is in the sovereign Ruler and King over all. Look into His eyes! Fix your gaze on Him! This is where our courage lies.

There is also the courage to do what is right. What is right is to forgive. This is what I am to choose. No excuses! No reasons for not doing it! Reach down deep, draw upon the resurrected life of Christ, step out, and do the right thing. We possess great power. What is that quote? "With great power comes great responsibility." Our responsibility is to forgive. In the new *Amazing Spider-Man*, the quote is changed and Uncle Ben actually tells Peter Parker that it is not a choice to do what is right but it is our responsibility. We are under the orders of our King. Our responsibility is to obey.

Finally, we need the courage to suffer hurt. Yep, that's right! Things aren't always going to work out the way we envision them. Just because we give forgiveness, it doesn't mean the person we give it to is going to jump into our arms. The person might not even think he has done anything wrong or needs to be forgiven at all. He might look you in the eyes and tell you that he will never forgive you or never ask you to forgive him (been there, had both of those responses). Again, we do not do this, ultimately, for them. We are doing it for the glory and honor of Christ, and we know that our own inner man desperately needs it.

Chapter 5

The Final Thing

We have been focusing mainly on the importance and necessity of giving forgiveness. At the same time, we need to mention that we take the initiative to ask others to forgive us. All of us are to be in tune with our own wrong thoughts, wrong motives, wrong attitudes, wrong words, and wrong actions. In fact, the prayer at the end of Psalm 139 is very instructive: "Search me, O God, and know my heart; try me and know my anxious thoughts; and see if there be any hurtful way in me, and lead me in the everlasting way" (vv. 23–24).

One of our greatest concerns is whether we have, in any way, offended someone else. So often, we are thinking about what someone has done to us and lose sight of the fact that we are people who are always in a spiritual battle with our own self-centered thoughts and concerns. Our rights become our priority. What we aspire to often gets in the way of walking uprightly "with all humility and gentleness, with patience, showing forbearance to one another in love ..." (Ephesians 4:2).

Before getting to the "final thing," a few disclaimers need to be addressed. First, it is one of the principles in writing that you stay with the same pronoun throughout the body of work being presented, and in most cases, it is preferred that the all-inclusive *we* is used so that everyone is being addressed and no one individual is being singled out. I have purposefully not done this. In fact, I go back and forth between we, you, and I. Sometimes things are so personal in what is being said that I use *I* intentionally. At other times, it is my intent to address *you*, the reader, in a way that you know I really want you to think about this and apply it to your life. So, if this offends *you*, I am sorry.

Second, there is no extensive bibliography at the end of what I have written. Whatever you might need in order to find a quote or a Scripture passage is contained within the paragraphs themselves. The majority of this material is my own as I have prayed over passages and wrestled with applying them to my own life and heart.

Third, I want to stress here that all of what I have written here has come from my own personal struggle in the area of forgiveness. I know what it is not to be forgiven. I know what it is for those who are your closest loved ones to say they have forgiven you, and yet you can see in the look that they give you they still consider you stained by what you have done and they are not about to let you have the same place in their lives that you had before. Also, I have had that personal battle with knowing that I should forgive and yet not wanting to forgive. The guy who I still consider to be my accountability partner, and one who has loved me in the midst of my greatest battles, after reading some of what I have written here, e-mailed me, "I don't believe I have ever really forgiven anyone." Amen! Been there too! It is the fight of my life.

Nothing I have said is easy. I know that. I want you to know that I know that and that nothing I have said here assumes that we are just going to jump up tomorrow and throw forgiveness around like a piece of paper rolled up into a ball. We have three strong enemies—the world, the Devil, and our own flesh—that are determined to keep us from being obedient to our heavenly Father. The battle is on! Awake or asleep, there is no quarter given.

Finally, I just want us to look at our definition of forgiveness one last time: *Forgiveness is the supernatural work of God's Spirit causing a person to choose to courageously set aside a wrong suffered, given freely and humbly, having been overwhelmed by the forgiveness one has received through the cross of Christ and done solely for Christ's glory and honor, no matter what has been done or who has done it.* Not everything can be stated in one brief statement about forgiveness. I am sure that you, the reader, would add things to this definition and may even wish to remove things. It is my purpose not to be exhaustive but to set forth the major premise of all that I have tried to say. We need a definition. There must be truth in regard to this great issue that we hold ourselves to and seek to accomplish as we live in relationship with other people. It is my hope and prayer that such a definition will help all of us offer freedom and release to those within our sphere of influence.

So what is the final thing? Pray with me! Yes, that's it! I want us to pray together. I am going to write out my own here. You can use my words, or it will probably be better for you to write out your own. This is your "homework." Pray! Then pray some more!

Here is my feeble attempt to enter the great throne of grace through the blood of Christ:

Oh, almighty, eternal, glorious Father, the God of all creation, Maker of the heavens and the earth, I come into Your presence seeking Your face and desiring nothing else but You. I come acknowledging the deep darkness and blackness of my heart. I have no right to even be here except I plead the merit and work of King Jesus on my behalf. I cannot forgive those who have trespassed against me. My heart is too Hard, and I only want harm to come to them. I am filled with bitterness hatred, anger, malice, and a desire for their utter destruction. Oh, Lord, I know this is wrong. I know that I must set all this aside. Forgive me for my inability to forgive. By the power of Your Holy Spirit, give me the power and the grace, even now, to dig that grave and to cast everything that I feel this other person has done to me into that pit and cover it over with Your patience, gentleness, humility, love, peace, and self-control. Come in all of Your power, overwhelm my inner man. Make me like Christ. Supernaturally enable me to give complete and unconditional forgiveness to

_____.

In the name of and for the sake of my Savior and Redeemer, amen.

It is the gospel that must free us. It is the glorious truth that, in the midst of my terrible nature that is opposed to the living and true God, and all my sins that proceed from it, Jesus Christ, the Son of God, came into this world, lived a perfect life, died a criminal's death, rose again from the dead, ascended to heaven, and sits on the right hand of God Most High. God's Holy Spirit makes me alive to all that He has done for me in Christ Jesus, gives me a new nature, causes faith and repentance to be produced in me, comes to live within me, and enables me to live a life that seeks to honor and glorify the One who has redeemed me. I know that I am forgiven, and it is my joy and honor to extend that forgiveness to others.

In light of all that is ours in Christ Jesus, worship with me:

> *Sing a new song to the LORD!*
>> *Let the whole earth sing to the Lord!*
> *Each day proclaim the good news that he saves.*
>> *Publish his glorious deeds among the nations.*
> *Tell everyone about the amazing things he does.*
>> *Great is the LORD! He is most worth of praise!*
> *The gods of other nations are mere idols,*
>> *but the LORD made the heavens!*
> *Honor and majesty surround him;*
>> *strength and beauty fill his sanctuary.*
>
> *O nations of the world, recognize the LORD;*
>> *recognize that the LORD is glorious and strong.*
> *Give to the LORD the glory he deserves!*
>> *Bring your offering and come into his courts*
> *Worship the LORD in all his holy splendor.*
>> *Let all the earth tremble before him.*
> *Tell all the nations, "The LORD reigns!"*
>> *The world stands firm and cannot be shaken.*
> *He will judge all peoples fairly.*

Let the heavens be glad, and the earth rejoice!

   Let the sea and everything in it shout his praise!

Let the fields and their crops bust out with joy!

   Let the trees of the forest rustle with praise

before the LORD, for he is coming!

   He is coming to judge the earth.

He will judge the world with justice,

   and the nations with his truth.

(Psalm 96, *New Living Translation,* Tyndale House Publishers, Inc., Carol Stream, Ill)